The Magic of Being Different

By Danielle Marie Chelvaratnam

The Magic of Being Different © Danielle Marie Chelvaratnam 2023

www.daniellemarie.au

The moral rights of Danielle Chelvaratnam to be identified as the author of this work have been asserted in accordance with the Copyright Act 1968.

First published in Australia 2023 by Danielle Chelvaratnam, Media 27.

Illustrations by Daria Fedchenko

ISBN 978-0-646-88274-1

Any opinions expressed in this work are exclusively those of the author and are not necessarily the views held or endorsed by Danielle Chelvaratnam.

All rights reserved. No part of this publication may be reproduced or transmitted by any means, electronic, photocopying or otherwise, without prior written permission of the author.

Disclaimer
All the information, techniques, skills and concepts contained within this publication are of the nature of general comment only, and are not in any way recommended as individual advice. The intent is to offer a variety of information to provide a wider range of choices now and in the future, recognising that we all have widely diverse circumstances and viewpoints. Should any reader choose to make use of the information herein, this is their decision, and the author and publisher/s do not assume any responsibilities whatsoever under any conditions or circumstances. The author does not take responsibility for the business, financial, personal or other success, results or fulfilment upon the readers' decision to use this information. It is recommended that the reader obtain their own independent advice.

This Book Belongs To

_____

_____

I love you but I also love me.
Being so different is a fun way to be!

Everybody is so different - this is exciting, just so great.

Imagine we all had the same colour skin and the same looking face?
Would you be able to remember who is Mia, Levi or Chase?

I love who I am, I'm so different, this is me.

I love who you are, so different to me.

I love my brown, straight hair, and your curly red hair is so you! I love that we're all so different. Don't you think so too?

Sometimes I wear my hair up, sometimes I like it down. How do you like to wear yours? Maybe crazy or with a crown!

My friend Liam, he's seven, he's really so tall.
I'm also seven, but much shorter overall.
We're all different, in every shape and way,
but we're friends, and that's what matters every day.

I can reach your toy in a small tight space.

And my friend Liam can catch your ball when you try and throw it into space.

Look at me, I have a scar from when the doctor fixed my heart.

My friend doesn't have a scar, but this doesn't set us apart.

I like to make up stories that I was bitten by a crocodile.

It's fun to share jokes about my scar once in a while.

I need to wear these glasses because they help me to see.

My friend doesn't wear them, because she doesn't need them like me.

I know my new green glasses are just something I need.

Aren't they cool? And I love it so much that now I can read!

Stop right here and point out all the things you like.

It's okay if you like the building blocks, the book, or the bike.

And don't worry if what you like is not there.

Maybe more than anything, you love your own teddy bear?

Maybe you can draw it and hold it up to share?

I love basketball, and my brother loves dolls.

We both love pink, and that's how we roll!

Don't you love that I can be me,
and you can be you?

What's your favourite game?
Do you love pink too?

Guess what? We are twins, and yes, we look the same.

But I bet you didn't know we don't like playing the same game.

So, I love to read, and my brother loves to play football.

And that's fine because we are all so different, after all.

Some of my friends have a different skin colour than mine.
Being so different means all of us get to shine.

I have lots and lots of freckles, but my brother only has a few.
I love how we look so different. Don't you think so too?

My best friend is good at maths, and I'm pretty good at art.
I think it's cool that both of us have our own kind of smart.

You may be great at music, or perhaps story writing.
You could be good at dancing, running, or even climbing.

We are all good at something, and I know you'll find your way because we have our own kind of smart in our own special way.

Oh, and there is one thing that I really know to be the same. We all are so beautiful in our own different ways.

I love you, but I also love me.
Being so different is a fun way to be!

Parent | Teacher Guide

All children deserve to go through life having fun, playing, and relaxing because enjoying life in a simple way plays a big role in healthy brain development. It is a shared desire for us all to see our kids happy and enjoying life. As a parent, my first experience of fearing for my child's happiness came when they started school. Every day, I would be filled with anxiety, questioning whether they were happy, making friends, and enjoying their time at school. This anxiety stemmed from my own unhappy school years, which were far from ideal.

As a mother of two young children and one young adult, my personal experiences have led me to dedicate my time to finding ways to promote happiness, prevent trauma, and encourage self-love and love for others, irrespective of appearance or race. When I look at my children, I want nothing but the best for them, as all parents do. We want them to be happy, and we certainly don't want them to be scared. Childhood should be a joyful time, although there will inevitably be challenges along the way, we hope that fear doesn't overshadow their experiences.

Originally, I wrote this book with the intention of helping my own children. As an Australian woman married to a Sri Lankan man, our family embraces diversity, encompassing differences in skin colour, looks, and race. It is essential to me that each child appreciates and loves their unique qualities, while also valuing and embracing the differences in those around them.

Having been teased during my own school years for being different, I experienced the negative impact it had on my mental health. I did not want my children to face bullying, nor did I want them to become bullies themselves. Mental health is a significant issue today, and I believe we can all take steps to ensure that children lead happier, healthier lives. From a young age, my own mental health suffered. In primary school, I endured teasing and name-calling, with children ridiculing my lips and resorting to physical violence, throwing me against walls and kicking me. Filled with fear, I chose not to confide in anyone—neither my teachers nor my parents—afraid that speaking up would only worsen the situation. Unfortunately, things neither improved nor worsened; they simply remained the same. The only respite I found was when my parents divorced, and my mother relocated us to a small country town, where I spent my final year of primary school among a handful of children. It was one of the few times I truly enjoyed school and formed lasting friendships. However, a few years later, our family returned to the city, and I attended a local high school, where the name-calling resumed. It all began when my brother wore his cowboy hat to school, proudly displaying his rural background. His peers began calling him 'cow patty', and upon discovering that I was his younger sister, they referred to me as 'calf patty'. Once again, fear gripped me, and I was terrified. The teasing shifted from mocking my brother's differences to targeting my acne. The impact on my mental health was worse than ever before. During high school, all I yearned for was acceptance, the feeling of beauty, and fitting in, just like any other teenager. However, I felt anything but those things. Instead, I felt fear, pain, ugliness, loneliness, and exclusion. School became unbearable, and I reached a point where I even tried taking my own life. This experience left a lasting  impact on my mental health and self-acceptance, which I struggled with until my mid-30s when I finally found the strength to address my fears. It took over 30 years for me to truly love and accept myself, embracing every aspect of who I am and accepting the skin I'm in. This awakening led me to dedicate my life to helping others feel comfortable in their own skin.

   I never, ever want my children to endure what I went through, and I never want them to treat others as I was treated. When I heard my six-year-old daughter making concerning comments about her skin colour, I realised that it was crucial to take action. That's when I decided to write this book for her. While there are many books available that aim to help children and adults love themselves, I firmly believe that it is equally important for individuals to love and respect others. Bullying must be eradicated, and as a parent, I am committed to doing whatever I can to shape my children into kind individuals. I understand that moulding our kids into confident and compassionate human beings begins with us, as parents and teachers. Therefore, the objective of this book is to assist your children in loving the skin they were born in, embracing their differences, and loving and respecting their peers at school or in any other setting. Together, let's help children see their differences in a positive light, filled with fun and brightness. After all, who determines what is beautiful? Who gets to decide the perfect nose shape, eye shape, or lip size? What constitutes the perfect skin colour, hair type, or facial structure? True beauty lies in embracing our differences, and this applies to all of us, not just our children.

   Let us all embrace our natural beauty!

The Importance of Acceptance & Self-Love

The value of self-acceptance and self-love in children cannot be overstated. When children possess a genuine love for themselves and a healthy self-esteem, they are more likely to exhibit the confidence necessary to explore new opportunities and persevere through challenges, even when things don't go as planned—an inevitable part of life. In contrast, children with low self-esteem often feel uncertain and may believe they are incapable of performing tasks well, leading them to give up prematurely or refrain from trying at all.

This concept of self-esteem extends to body confidence as well. Children with a healthy self-esteem are less prone to harbouring negative feelings about their bodies, provided they are consistently encouraged to love and appreciate themselves. It is crucial to remember that young children do not naturally focus on perceived flaws in their bodies or achievements unless these aspects are pointed out to them.

As parents and teachers, we hold the power to nurture and reinforce a child's healthy self-esteem by celebrating their accomplishments, regardless of size or significance. By transforming their 'I cant's' into 'I cans', we can instil in them the belief that they have the capability to attempt new things. We can encourage them to identify and appreciate the unique qualities of their bodies and why they should be cherished.

It is vital to recognise that we, as parents and teachers, are the most influential figures in our children's lives. They look up to us and often mirror our behaviours. If we fail to exhibit kindness and self-acceptance, if we are unable to look in the mirror and speak positively about ourselves, what chance do our children have to embrace and accept all aspects of themselves, including the natural changes that occur in their bodies throughout life's journey? Furthermore, what likelihood do they have of treating others with compassion if they perceive these changes as negative? We must remember that we are the primary role models in their lives, and our words and actions toward ourselves and others will shape their choices and behaviours as they navigate through life.

It is evident that fostering acceptance and self-love in children is not only essential for their well-being but also holds the power to shape their future with confidence and compassion.

Activities you can do with your child/children at home or in the classroom

Positive Self-Love Flower

An activity that children absolutely love! This activity is designed to boost their self-esteem and foster a positive self-image. Even if your child is still learning to write, you can be their helping hand in this empowering experience.

To begin, draw a simple flower with petals. In the centre, write 'I am'. Now, encourage your child to come up with positive affirmations about themselves and write them on each petal. You can join in and share your own positive affirmations as well. This creates a beautiful opportunity for conversation and connection.

For instance, if they write 'I am brave' you can say, 'Tell me about being brave. What makes you brave?' This prompts your child to reflect on their own strengths and qualities, cultivating a sense of pride and self-awareness.

Another fantastic variation of this activity is to focus on someone else. Instead of 'I am', write the name of a peer in your child's class in the centre of the flower. For example, 'Mia is...'. Then, ask your child to think of positive qualities about their friend and write them on the petals. This not only encourages appreciation for others but also reinforces the idea of lifting each other up and celebrating the goodness in everyone.

The Positive Self-Love Flower is a powerful tool to nurture self-esteem and spread positivity. By engaging in this activity, children learn to value their own unique qualities and recognise the strengths of those around them. It's a beautiful way to cultivate kindness, self-acceptance, and a supportive classroom environment.

So, gather your art supplies and embark on this joyful adventure with your child. Let the Positive Self-Love Flower bloom, filling their hearts with confidence, compassion, and a deep appreciation for themselves and others.

5 Things I Love About Myself

This engaging activity can be enjoyed at home or in the classroom, offering children an opportunity to express and celebrate their unique qualities. It also allows them to focus on aspects of their bodies, such as eye colour or hair type. Additionally, this activity can be adapted to appreciate someone else, such as a sibling or a friend.

Instructions:

1. Provide each child with a sheet of paper and writing materials. You can photocopy this print at the end of this book.

2. Encourage them to think about what makes them special and unique.

3. Instruct them to write down five things they love about themselves, paying attention to physical attributes if desired.

4. Emphasise that these qualities can be anything they appreciate.

5. For added creativity, suggest using descriptive language or drawing accompanying illustrations.

6. Optionally, if doing the activity about someone else, prompt them to write down five things they love about a sibling, friend, or another person in their life.

7. Once completed, allow the children to share their lists, fostering a positive and supportive environment.

This activity encourages self-reflection, self-acceptance, and appreciation for individuality. It helps children develop a positive mindset and cultivates a sense of self-love. By extending the activity to others, it promotes kindness, empathy, and recognition of the unique qualities in those around them.

Remember, the goal of this activity is to foster a positive self-image and encourage children to embrace their own and others' differences with love and respect.

The Magic of Kindness

This impactful activity promotes a positive and inclusive classroom environment by encouraging children to focus on the strengths and qualities of their classmates, even in situations where conflicts may have arisen. It can be easily conducted both at home and in the classroom, fostering a sense of unity and appreciation among children.

Instructions:

1. Prepare several sheets of butcher's paper and write each child's name at the top of a separate sheet.

2. Display the sheets around the classroom, making them easily accessible to all children.

3. Explain to the children that they will be participating in a special activity called - The Magic of Kindness.

4. Encourage each child to move around the classroom, taking turns visiting each sheet of paper.

5. Instruct them to write down one positive thing or quality they appreciate about the named child under their respective names.

6. Emphasise that it is essential to find something positive for every child, regardless of any past conflicts or differences.

7. Encourage creativity and variety in their responses, such as highlighting acts of kindness, personal strengths, or unique talents.

8. Provide support and guidance as needed, ensuring that each child feels comfortable and included throughout the activity.

9. Once everyone has contributed to each sheet, gather the children together for a discussion about the power of kindness and the positive impact it can have on individuals and the entire classroom.

10. Take a moment to celebrate the kind words written about each child, fostering a warm and supportive environment.

This activity cultivates empathy, kindness, and a sense of belonging among children. It allows them to recognise and appreciate the diverse qualities and strengths that each individual brings to the classroom. By encouraging children to find positive aspects about their peers, even in challenging situations, they learn the value of understanding, respect, and unity.

Remember, the Magic of Kindness activity creates an opportunity for children to uplift and inspire each other, fostering a culture of empathy and positivity within the classroom.

'I Love Me' Jar

This engaging activity encourages children to foster self-love and positive self-talk on a daily basis. Whether conducted at home or in the classroom, the 'I Love Me' Jar provides a tangible reminder of their unique qualities and self-appreciation.

Instructions:

1. Begin by having each child decorate a jar using their preferred artistic materials. They can unleash their creativity and personalise the jar in any way they like.

2. Write 'I Love Me' or any other affirming phrase on the jar to emphasise its purpose.

3. Explain to the children that the jar will serve as a daily reminder of what they appreciate about themselves.

4. Encourage them to reflect on and identify positive aspects about themselves, such as their talents, physical appearances, accomplishments, or acts of kindness.

5. Each day, provide a small piece of paper or sticky note for the child to write down something they love about themselves.

6. Prompt them to fold the note and place it into the jar.

7. Encourage consistency by repeating this activity for a week or two, allowing the jar to gradually fill with notes of self-appreciation.

8. Remind the children to read the notes in the jar periodically, serving as a continuous reminder of their self-worth and the positive qualities they possess.

The 'I Love Me' Jar activity enables children to cultivate a habit of positive self-talk and self-affirmation. By encouraging them to identify and appreciate their unique attributes, the activity promotes self-love and boosts self-esteem. It serves as a powerful tool in fostering a positive mindset and encouraging children to recognise and celebrate their own worth.

Whether at home or in the classroom, this activity helps create a nurturing environment that values self-acceptance, resilience, and personal growth. It serves as a visual reminder for children to cherish themselves and embrace their individuality, fostering a lifelong habit of self-love and positivity.

The Kindness Mirror

This activity is aimed to encourage self-love, build empathy, and celebrate both the uniqueness and similarities among classmates. Start by discussing the concept of self-love and kindness with the children. Explain that kindness begins with being kind to ourselves. Use relatable examples and simple language.

Instructions:

1. Creating a 'Kindness Mirror': Give each child an unbreakable mirror to decorate. You can find small mirrors at craft stores or use plastic mirrors. They can use markers, stickers, or colored paper to make it unique.

2. Reflecting on Individuality: Have children sit in a circle and ask each child to look into their mirrors, then ask them to share something they really like about themselves. It could be a physical feature, a talent, or something they're good at.

3. Kindness Mirror Wall: Provide a large poster paper or bulletin board. Ask each child has to tape or glue their decorated mirror onto the poster paper, creating a 'Kindness Mirror Wall'. You can write each child's name above their mirror.

4. Embracing Uniqueness: Discuss the uniqueness of each mirror, emphasising that people are unique too, and that's what makes them special.

5. Acts of Kindness Challenge: Encourage kindness in the classroom. Explain that kindness is not only about being kind to ourselves but also to others. Encourage the children to perform acts of kindness in the classroom. It could be helping a friend, sharing, or saying something nice. Whenever a child does an act of kindness, they can add a star or a heart sticker next to their mirror on the 'Kindness Mirror Wall'.

6. Daily Reflection: Dedicate a few minutes each day for the children to look at their mirrors and say one kind thing about themselves. Encourage them to compliment their classmates too.

This activity can also be done at home, making it a great opportunity for parents to join in. It helps children develop self-esteem, practice kindness, and celebrate both their individuality and the unique qualities of their peers/siblings. This, in turn, fosters a positive and supportive environment while promoting self-love and empathy.

Positive Affirmations for Kids

Positive affirmations have a powerful impact on creating a nurturing environment, both at home and in the classroom. By surrounding ourselves with uplifting words, we reinforce the belief that we are capable and deserving. Encouraging children to embrace positive affirmations can boost their self-esteem and instil a sense of self-worth. Here are some affirmations that can be printed and displayed in your home or classroom:

- I am brave.
- I am smart.
- I am strong.
- I am creative.
- I am unique.
- I am kind.
- I am loved.
- I am enough.
- I am beautiful.

By incorporating affirmations into their daily lives, they cultivate a strong foundation of self-belief and resilience. Positive affirmations help children recognize their worth, embrace their individuality, and foster a mindset of kindness and compassion towards themselves and others.

A Little Note:

I want you to remember this: we are all unique and beautiful in our own way. You are more than enough—beautiful, smart, and capable of bravery. The same goes for your child or children. Look deep within and embrace this truth. When we accept it within ourselves, we empower our children to do the same. Each person's individuality is what makes this world so beautiful. Never forget that. Together, one step at a time, we can change the world.

5 Things that I LOVE about myself

1. _____
2. _____
3. _____
4. _____
5. _____

NOTES

www.ingramcontent.com/pod-product-compliance
Lightning Source LLC
Chambersburg PA
CBHW061800290426
44109CB00030B/2907